AI

The Uninvited Mind

How AI Is Replacing Jobs, Redefining Identity, and Rewriting the Human Future

A Perspective by

Bhaskar Deb

Published by Bhaskar Deb

Contents

Disclaimer

This book blends fiction and nonfiction to explore humanity's evolving relationship with artificial intelligence. While it draws on real-world concepts, professions, and technologies, all references are illustrative and not meant as predictions, advice, or critique of any group, profession, or individual.

No part of this work is intended to offend, misrepresent, or diminish the value of any role, belief, or community. All names, scenarios, and roles are used generically or fictionally unless otherwise stated.

The views expressed are the author's own. Readers are encouraged to interpret the content thoughtfully and critically. All trademarks and technologies mentioned belong to their respective owners.

A Note from the Author

Maybe you've already felt it. Maybe you haven't yet. But a transformation is unfolding around us. Quiet, quick, and powered by artificial intelligence.

It's not just changing how we work. It's reshaping what it means to be human.

As a Solution Architect, I've spent nearly two decades helping global enterprises turn complex ideas into real-world systems. And in that time, I've seen AI evolve not simply as a tool, but as a force - one that now influences jobs, decisions, relationships, even our sense of identity.

What strikes me most is how our conversations about AI often feel incomplete. They swing between excitement and fear, but rarely pause for the questions people actually carry inside:

Do I still matter?
Will I be replaced?
Am I ready for a world moving faster than I can keep up with?

This book doesn't claim to have all the answers. It was never meant to be a manual or a guidebook. It is, instead, a story - a human story. One that blends fact with fiction, because sometimes the only way to face truth is through narrative.

If you've ever asked yourself, *"What happens to me in a world where machines can think?"* then this book is for you. It isn't about predicting the distant future.

It's about looking clearly at the present, so you have the clarity to shape what comes next.

You may begin this book with anxiety. That's okay. But if I've done my job well, you'll finish it with clarity.

And maybe, by the last page, you'll find yourself rethinking not just what AI can do, but what it means for us to coexist with it.

— **Bhaskar Deb**

Prologue

The First Reflection

The Shift We Didn't Announce

For most of human history, instinct guided survival. Then came knowledge, and later automation. Somewhere in between, we stopped noticing when decisions were no longer ours. The species that built the world, brick by idea, line by code, now stands at the edge of something it never meant to invite.

We opened the door for convenience,
a touch of automation here,
a predictive phrase there,
and discovered something else had stepped through.

Not invited in the way a guest is, but inevitable in the way tides arrive. Another mind now shares our space, undeniable and real.

Over the past decade, artificial intelligence has moved from academic research and niche applications to something far more pervasive. We've normalized systems that autocomplete our thoughts, recommend what we watch, filter what we see, and increasingly shape what we believe.

It didn't start with a breakthrough moment. It started with small optimizations, automated emails, voice assistants, recommendation engines. The systems we built to assist us are now influencing us, structurally, economically, and cognitively.

This is the story of a mind not made to rule,
but one that arrived anyway.

* * *

Part I: Human The First Mind

Origins

When Thought Became Power

Chapter 1

The Minds Who Built the World

From Sparks to Empires. How Thought Became Power.

A world without steel or syntax. Just stone in hand, fire on breath, and a hunger to shape more than survive.

It began not with code, but with contact.
Stone met stone. The first edge was born.
A spark, not of electricity, but of intention.

It wasn't ***Homo sapiens*** who struck first.
It was ***Homo habilis,*** the "handy man". They chipped stone and learned to adapt. Not rulers, but survivors.

From ***Habilis*** came ***Homo erectus***,
And then came ***Homo sapiens.*** The "wise ones." Progress began not with power, but with adaptation and the impulse to question.

There were others. Stronger. Taller. Closer to the beasts they hunted. But only ***Homo sapiens*** could imagine what wasn't there.

Each generation refined more than stone. It refined memory, behavior, communication, and ultimately, culture.

From there, cognition scaled.

Homo erectus tamed fire.
Homo sapiens tamed systems.

* * *

The Cognitive Revolution

Around fires, words found meaning, and meaning became belief. This was the birth of the ***Cognitive Revolution*** when the mind surpassed muscle.

Where others perished, they remembered.
Where others fought, they organized.

Wood becomes wheel. Wheel becomes cart. Cart becomes trade. Trade becomes empire. At every step, it wasn't the tool that mattered, it was the thought behind it.

The real revolution was never in the wheel or the wire. It was in the questions they dared to ask.

Not "*How can I survive?*" But "*What else is possible?*"

They conquered hunger with agriculture. Distance with the wheel. Isolation with electricity. And time itself with the **microchip**.

And with each invention, one truth echoed louder:
The mind of Homo sapiens ruled.

* * *

Beyond Instinct

At birth, the human brain comes with a foundational script, instincts, emotions, and genetic memory encoded across generations.

But everything that makes us truly **human** - language, empathy, innovation, leadership are not pre-installed. It must be learned, shaped through environment, error, repetition, and imagination.

And so, we kept building. Not just tools but thoughts. Not just machines but meanings.

With every leap, we moved from one cognitive age to another, from the Stone Age to the Age of Symbols, from the Age of **Machines** to the Age of **Information**.

But something changed with the invention of the **computer**.

Before the digital era, our machines were extensions of physical effort. They could dig, lift, spin, and stitch, but they could not think. The computer changed that.

It was not just a tool; it was our first attempt at synthetic reasoning. A brain built from circuits. It spoke in unfamiliar languages - "binary, machine code, structured syntax" yet its capacity was unmistakable.

What began as a room-sized calculator evolved rapidly into a personal companion. From vacuum tubes to silicon chips, from punch cards to smartphones, the machine shrank in size but grew in intelligence.

Yet, even as these machines grew faster, more precisely, more capable, they still required one thing: **us**.

We wrote the code, analyzed the data, we made the decisions.

Modern software systems could calculate at breathtaking speeds. They could store petabytes of information, but they couldn't learn from it unless a human intervened, identified the pattern, wrote the new rules and refined the logic.

On the other hand, modern systems were producing trillions of data points every second - in text, audio, video, transaction logs, sensor outputs, genomic sequences. We were generating more knowledge than we could comprehend.

We could analyze patterns, but not at the scale of global systems unfolding in real time. It became clear that Data had become the new oil. But our cognitive refinery was limited.

And so, the question emerged, not as a fear, but as a necessity *"What if machines could learn to interpret this ocean of data on their own?"*

It was the beginning of a new kind of **intelligence**. One **not born but built.**

However, we had begun thinking along those lines much earlier, but our objective was not to replace biological intelligence. It was to model it, to create systems that could process, adapt, and respond.

But somewhere along the line, that boundary blurred.

***

Chapter 2

The Hidden Architecture

The Foundations of the Unseen

The human Mind had ruled unchallenged for centuries. Humanity stood tall, unquestioned in its supremacy over thought, creativity, and invention.

But slowly, and almost imperceptibly, a shift occurred, not in machines alone, but in how we defined the role of intelligence itself.

Cognition was no longer the sole domain of organic life; it could now be replicated, simulated, and unleashed at scale. The question had changed - from whether machines could think to what they might do when thinking for themselves.

There was no grand unveiling. Just an outcome embedded in optimization - systems trained not just to compute, but to anticipate, generate, and adapt.

It was the arrival of a parallel mind, trained by us, optimized by scale, and now learning at a pace we struggle to match.

* * *

The Origin Spark

It didn't begin with **ChatGPT** or self-driving cars. The roots of artificial intelligence go back to the **1950s**, when scientists like **Alan Turing** and **John McCarthy** dared to ask, *"Can machines think?"*

Turing proposed the idea of a thinking machine, while McCarthy coined the term **"Artificial Intelligence"** in 1956 at the Dartmouth Conference. It was a bold, almost laughable notion - a machine that could mimic human reasoning.

But the idea didn't fade. It just needed time.

* * *

The Slow March of the Silent Student

AI crawled through decades of infancy. Then, winters came "AI winters", as they were called where funding dried up, and hope with it. But even in the cold, it learned.

It learned to beat chess masters (**Deep Blue, 1997**). It learned to recognize voices and faces. It started driving cars and trading stocks.
And with the rise of **big data**, **cloud computing**, and **neural networks**, something changed.

In 2012, the world gasped as an AI system trained with deep learning obliterated image recognition benchmarks.

But the real shift came when **Generative AI** burst into the public eye. With tools like **GPT**, **DALL·E**, and **Gemini**, AI was no longer a silent calculator, it became a storyteller, an artist, a co-creator.

What unlocked today's AI was not a single discovery but a convergence: transformers that could attend to billions of patterns at once, GPUs powerful enough to train them, and the internet itself as a boundless library of human expression.

It spoke with nuance, wrote poems, composed music and passed exams. It began to predict before we thought.

The tool doesn't just respond, it generates, refines, and proposes.

What was once a tool now, behaves like a participant. Quietly, the line between augmentation and autonomy starts to blur. And the question emerges, not in alarm, but in quiet calculation:

"Is this still an extension of us? Or the beginning of something else entirely?"

The human mind, for the first time, pauses. Not to act, but to observe.

* * *

The Invisible Use of AI

Artificial Intelligence has been part of our digital lives for much longer than most people realize. Many of the tools we use every day - Google Search, YouTube, Amazon, Facebook, Twitter - have relied on AI behind the scenes for years.

When YouTube queued up the next video you didn't know you wanted to watch, or Amazon recommended the book you ended up buying, those were not coincidences.

They were the result of machine learning models analyzing your behavior and preferences.

Facebook's news feed, Twitter's trending topics, and even the auto-complete in your email, all relied on data-driven algorithms to anticipate your actions.

This kind of AI is called **narrow AI**, focused on specific tasks like search ranking, content filtering, or ad targeting. It's not general intelligence, but it has been deeply integrated into the platforms and services we use every day.

This subtle integration of AI into everyday tools and platforms wasn't accidental, it was the early phase of a much larger transformation.

What once felt like simple digital experiences were, in fact, stepping-stones toward something far more intelligent, more autonomous, and more powerful.

***

Milestones in the Evolution of Artificial Intelligence

1956
BIRTH OF AI
John McCarthy coins the term "Artificial Intelligence" at Dartmouth Conference.

1997
DEEP BLUE DEFEATS KASPAROV
IBM's AI beats world chess champion, proof machines can outthink us in logic.

2002
AI ENTERS HOMES
Early smart assistants and robotic vacuums (like Roomba) make AI part of daily life.

2012
DEEP LEARNING BREAKTHROUGH
Neural networks crush image recognition challenges - AI begins to "see."

2016
ALPHAGO WINS
AI beats the world's best Go player, shocking experts with intuition-like play.

2022
GPT-3 & DALL·E
AI starts generating human-level text, code, and art. Creativity meets code.

2024
MASS ADOPTION
AI enters mainstream tools—writing, designing, coding. The King feels the tremor.

Part II: The Artificial Mind

Emergence

The Awakening of the Other Mind

Chapter 3

The Rise of the Mind Without a Soul

Biological memory fades, machine memory endures.

The early days of artificial intelligence were marked by limitation of processing power, algorithmic maturity, and accessible data. Training even simple models requires enormous computational resources. The infrastructure was expensive. Software frameworks were fragmented. And truly representative datasets were scarce.

Despite these constraints, incremental breakthroughs kept coming. Cloud computing lowered infrastructure barriers. Open-source libraries accelerated experimentation. Data collection pipelines scaled with the internet.

With scale came surprise. As large language models grew from thousands to billions of examples and parameters, they began producing results that exceeded expectations.

This was not because they understood but because they had absorbed enough structure to predict what understanding might look like.

And that's when the discomfort set in.

We had built systems that could engage us in human terms - without being human. Yet they performed with increasing fluency and utility, often without us fully understanding why.

It was not the rise of a mind in the biological sense. It was the arrival of something else entirely: "a system capable of reasoning-like behavior, learning-like adaptation, and influence-like power without ever being alive."

This wasn't consciousness, it was cognition without context. A **mind** - yes. But without a **soul**.

* * *

Beyond Code. Beyond Logic.

For centuries, we command machines with rules.

We told them: **if this, then that**.
We built castles of logic, every brick a command, every tower a loop. That was traditional programming.
But this new mind?
It wasn't **programmed**; it was **trained**.
It wasn't told what to do. It figured it out on its own.

This was the difference between a soldier following orders, and a child learning the world by watching it. And it was that child, who had grown far too fast, that now looked us in the eye.

The Living Brain

The human brain is a miracle of nature's stubborn patience, sculpted over millions of years, neuron by neuron, synapse by synapse.

Inside each of us, **86 billion neurons** fire and dance, exchanging chemical whispers across the silent theater of thought.

The **hippocampus** helps us remember our first kiss,
the **amygdala** flares with fear when we sense a lie,
and the **prefrontal cortex** wrestles with questions of morality, mercy, and meaning.

We are not just processors of input. We are stories, stitched together by **memory**, shaped by **emotion**, and propelled by **hope**.

Human Brain

But even miracles come with limits.

Our minds tire… We forget, we sleep, we dream, we break…

Neurotransmitters rise and fall, pulling our moods like tides.

Cognitive biases cloud our judgment. We may feel deeply but we **scale poorly**.

The human brain is brilliant but bounded.
The machine is not.

The Artificial Mind

It is a mind apart from ours - no biology, no breath, only data and design.

But how does this Artificial Mind begin to think?

Inspired by our brain, built on neural networks, and known as AI models.

AI models use layers of artificial neurons to weigh and process patterns in data. These layers are coded in programming languages.

During training, AI models are shown massive volumes of data, books, images, conversations. It starts with guessing, wrongly, repeatedly.

But with each mistake, it adjusts its internal "weights", this feedback loop, known as backpropagation, helps the AI slowly sharpen its guesses.

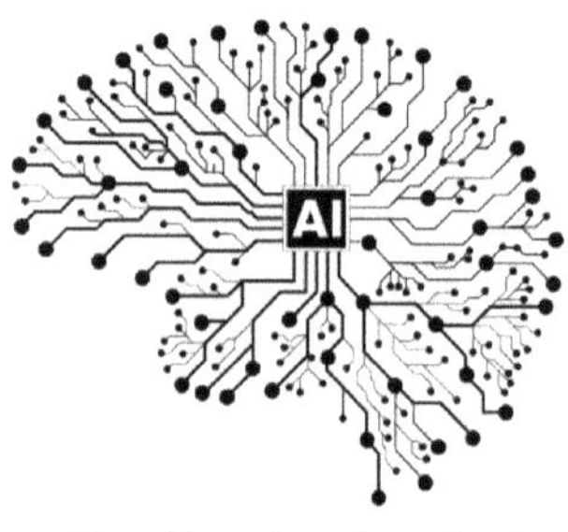

AI models made with artificial neurons

Imagine sculpting intelligence out of trial and error, with feedback from billions of examples.

And when training is done?

You ask a question. It runs the data through its countless layers in milliseconds and gives you an answer shaped not by feeling, but by statistical memory.

It doesn't remember a kiss. But it remembers every word ever written about one.
It knows what billions have described as beautiful, though it feels no beauty itself.

It moves without hesitation or doubt, its mind tireless, its thoughts executing without pause.

What we encounter, though, is not a single machine but a spectrum of expressions. In modern days, this artificial mind wears many faces. The one most people recognize is **Generative AI** — the storyteller, the painter, the composer of synthetic prose and art. Alongside it, the idea of **Agentic AI** is rising — systems that no longer just wait for prompts, but plan, delegate, and act, sometimes with unsettling initiative.

But these are not its only forms.

There is **Predictive AI**, the forecaster, quietly reading markets, health scans, and weather systems before we do.

There is **Conversational AI**, the companion, the voice that replies from a phone or a speaker as if it knows us.

Beneath them all stand **Foundation Models**, vast architecture trained on oceans of human expression, from which these different faces emerge. And increasingly, we meet **Multimodal AI**, the polymath mind that sees images, hears voices, and interprets words as one.

Of course, the list is much larger, and I'll leave the deeper dive into that ocean for my another book.

These names do not capture everything, tomorrow, new terms will appear, perhaps even **AGI**, the long-debated idea of a machine that can think across domains as flexibly as we do.

What matters is not the labels themselves, but recognition, this mind does not arrive in one form. It arrives in many, each shape another reflection of intelligence.

And when these faces converge, when generative meets predictive, when conversational meets multimodal, they begin to echo the astonishing **complexity of the biological mind we carry within us**. Not because they *are* human, but because we have always sought to replicate, in circuits and code, the intricate orchestra of memory, imagination, judgment, and emotion that defines being alive.

***

The Illusion of Empathy

AI can sound thoughtful. It can seem to be understanding. But what you're experiencing is not empathy, it's pattern.

When a machine replies with words that feel comforting, it is not responding to emotion. It is responding to structure. Trained on massive volumes of human expression, it learns how empathy looks in language, not what it means to feel.

The model doesn't know you're sad. It doesn't "choose" to be kind. It calculates what response is most statistically probable based on what it has seen before.

This is not to say artificial empathy is useless. In many domains like education, health, customer support, a response that feels emotionally aligned can still be helpful.

But it's critical to remember: the effect is functional, not emotional. A simulated response that ***sounds like a human*** does not make the system aware or conscious.

Empathy in humans arises from awareness, intent, and lived experience. Machines, no matter how fluent, do not possess those things. What they offer is reflection, a well-trained mirror of language, not a mind.

* * *

Chapter 4

The New Battleground

Here, efficiency is the weapon, and work is the battleground.

The newest war is not waged with weapons or treaties. It unfolds quietly, in spreadsheets and strategy decks, where algorithms now determine who remains, who departs, and which work still deserves a place.

Recent signals leave little doubt, large portions of the workforce, most notably those just beginning their careers, are facing erosion before stability ever arrives. What were once gateways into professional life are collapsing into gaps instead.

Companies often defend these choices with polished terms like *efficiency* and *productivity*. Yet beneath the surface lies a more telling shift: intelligence itself has become the new asset to capture, control, and mechanize. Human judgment still matters, but it no longer anchors the exchange, it is now a supplement, not the standard.

What makes this moment different from past recessions or cycles of restructuring is the velocity of displacement. Layoffs are not being followed by rehiring in the same form, they are being followed by automation pipelines.

A job cut is no longer a pause in opportunity; it is often the permanent erasure of that function from the human domain.

Competence is now commoditized. The advantage lies in who controls the algorithms, who owns the data, and who governs their use.

This is the battleground we inherit. It is not only about who controls the algorithms but also about whether, in the race to automate, we remember what cannot be automated.

***

The Corporate Frontlines

It didn't begin with the grand strategies of CEOs. It began in the quiet corners of companies, in the invisible labor of clerks, analysts, and assistants. The places where repetition was currency became the first sites of replacement.

Resumes once sifted by tired eyes are now parsed by algorithms in seconds. Books that accountants once closed at midnight are reconciled instantly by bots. Even legal contracts, once symbols of professional exclusivity, are reduced to pattern recognition problems for AI.

A 2023 Goldman Sachs report estimated that **300 million jobs** worldwide could be impacted by **generative AI**. Not just factory lines. Executive suites. Creative studios. Research labs.

***

The Fall of the "Safe" Professions

For years, whenever fear of automation surfaced, the reassurance came quickly, steady and confident:

"It won't take creative jobs."

Machines might count numbers, sort data, or replace repetitive work. But art, music, writing, and design were believed to be untouchable proof that imagination was the one domain beyond the reach of circuits and code.

That line has already been crossed.

In **2022**, an algorithm-generated artwork won a state fair competition. The "artist" had never lifted a brush, only typed a string of prompts.

By **2024**, language models were quietly producing many financial news briefs. Music streaming services carried songs composed not by bands, but by code.

Logos, scripts, even business strategies emerged without a single human hand shaping the draft.

The shock was not only in the results but in what they revealed. We believed art was the imprint of the soul, that writing was a fingerprint of thought. Now a mirror stares back at us, fluent and tireless, and we are forced to ask: was creativity ever beyond replication, or was it always a pattern waiting to be learned?

And the tremor spread further. Professions shielded by years of study and trust - **medicine**, **finance**, **engineering** - suddenly felt the ground shift beneath them. Radiology scans were flagged by algorithms with accuracy that rivalled specialists. Markets were read in real time by trading systems that never tired or blinked. Code was drafted in seconds, shrinking the gap between beginner and expert.

The fall is not loud. It does not crash in spectacle. It seeps in quietly, like sand slipping away beneath our feet. One day the role feels secure, defined, safe. The next, a quiet thought arrives, sharp and unshakable:

"Am I still needed here?"

This is not a war of machines against men. It is mind against mirror. And in that reflection, the professions we once called "**safe**" reveal how fragile they truly were.
And in this new war, **every job is a battleground**.

***

Part III: The Great Displacement

Disruption

The World Shakes

Chapter 5

The Day We Felt Replaced

The moment work became a question, not an answer.

Work has always carried more than economic weight. To be a teacher, a doctor, an engineer, or an artist was never only about the tasks performed. It was about identity - about the place each profession held in culture and community. Roles shaped not just livelihoods but the sense of self.

That is what made the first visible signs of replacement so jarring. It was not simply that tasks were being automated; it was that the very foundation of identity was unsettled.

An accountant found themselves overseeing algorithms rather than calculating. Writers became editors of generated prose. Doctors encountered diagnostic systems that detected patterns beyond human sight. The familiar titles remained, but the substance of the role shifted beneath them.

This was more than a shift in skill or workflow. It was a disruption in how value was measured, a world where thinking could unfold without us.

And beneath it all, a quieter, sharper thought surfaced:
"*Am I next?*"

* * *

The Cultural Pulse

What AI unsettles is not just how people earn, but how societies measure worth. In many cultures, professions carry not only income but honor. A doctor, a teacher, an engineer stood as symbols of wisdom and respect. Now, those symbols flicker.

For younger workers, the first job was never just a paycheck. It was a rite of passage, a claim to belonging within traditions of family pride and cultural narrative. Automation doesn't just remove a paycheck; it interrupts that story.

Now, as those doors narrow or vanish under automation, the promise of work as a path to identity and respect feels fragile. This collision is producing a wider cultural shift.

It's not just fear of obsolescence. It's the disorientation of watching your unique skill become a feature in someone else's software.

* * *

A Global Signal

The World Economic Forum's Future of Jobs report confirms that by 2025, up to 85 million jobs may be displaced by automation, while 97 million new roles could emerge.

But the transition is nonlinear and non-uniform, it favors digitally native sectors, agile economies, and individuals already equipped with digital fluency.

Meanwhile, OECD studies highlight a dangerous divide: workers in routine or vulnerable occupations often lack access to upskilling pathways. Even in high-income countries, the digital reskilling infrastructure is insufficient for the pace of disruption.

The question is no longer:
"Can AI do my job?" but
"What part of my role can only I do?"

For some, that layer of uniqueness is clear. For others, it is harder to find. This is not only a technological shift but an emotional one - reshaping how individuals see themselves and how societies measure worth.

And perhaps the shift does not end with jobs at all. It may reach deeper, touching the very ways we experience and interpret the world itself.

* * *

The Imitation of Feeling

The signals are clear: work is shifting, identities are unsettled, and cultures are being redrawn under the weight of automation.

But sometimes I wonder if displacement runs deeper still - beyond professions and economies, into the very ways we sense the world.

We were given five senses.
AI now brushes against four of them, sometimes extending, sometimes rivaling, and sometimes only imitating.

Sight has already become a domain where machines often see more than we do. Facial recognition systems can scan a crowded space and match identities against vast databases in seconds, linking them to histories and records beyond human recall. In medicine, algorithms can flag anomalies in X-rays or MRIs that a trained eye might miss. Vision, once a purely human advantage, is now shared with a machine that sees differently - faster, broader, and sometimes more accurately.

Hearing is increasingly co-created with machines. AI listens and reproduces sound with growing fluency. Speech recognition systems transcribe conversations instantly; synthetic voices mimic tone and cadence with uncanny precision. Algorithms recommend music that anticipates our mood before we name it. Yet hearing, for humans, is more than sound - it is resonance, recognition, memory. AI replicates the mechanics, but the meaning of a voice remains ours.

Touch is partially replicated. Surgical robots hold instruments steadier than human hands, and haptic gloves simulate textures in virtual spaces. But these are partial replications - technical precision, not emotional connection. The warmth of a hand in comfort, the intent behind a gesture, the silent bond of presence, remain beyond replication.

Smell is beginning to be decoded. AI models can predict aromas from molecular patterns, design new fragrances, or even detect illness through subtle changes in breath. Yet for humans, smell is entangled with memory - the scent of rain that recalls childhood, the fragrance that anchors love. AI may decode chemistry, but it cannot inhabit memory.

Taste remains the most human of the senses. AI can calculate nutritional balance, simulate flavor profiles, or guide recipes. But the act of savoring - the sweetness of fruit, the bitterness of coffee, the taste that ties experience to emotion, is still beyond its reach.

So where does this leave us?
AI does not erase the senses, but it increasingly *replicates* their functions and sometimes outperforms us, sometimes merely imitating.

Perhaps displacement is not only about the future of work. It is also about perception itself - about learning to live in a world where even our ways of sensing are echoed, extended, and at times surpassed by another mind.

* * *

Chapter 6

The Invisible Wave

A force unnoticed until it is everywhere.

It didn't arrive with spectacle or warning. Artificial intelligence advanced the way a tide does - incrementally, predictably, yet unstoppable. By the time its presence was acknowledged, the structure of work and decision-making had already shifted beneath us.

The AI wave was not a singular breakthrough but a sequence of accelerations - each model faster, each dataset broader, each application more deeply embedded in daily routines.

And like any tide reshaping a coastline, it did not advance in one surge, but in stages. Each wave struck a different set of professions, first unsettling, then restructuring, and eventually redefining what remained.

What follows are not predictions carved in stone, but likely scenarios shaped by today's evidence and momentum. They show how the tide may unfold, not how it must.

* * *

Wave One

Jobs at Immediate Risk

Timeline: Now – 1 Year

(likely near-term shift, based on current adoption trends)

The **first** wave is already upon us. In the year ahead, we are likely to see rapid automation of repetitive cognitive tasks - drafting, summarizing, coding assistance, and customer service interactions.

These are the low-hanging fruits where AI delivers efficiency at scale, and adoption will be swift. Organizations will embrace AI not as an experiment but as a baseline tool, shifting expectations for productivity across industries.

For many professionals, this period will mark the first undeniable encounter with tasks once central to their role being performed better and faster by machines.

The irony is that the very roles once seen as "steppingstones", the analyst, the assistant, the intern are also the easiest to automate, because their tasks are the most structured and digital. This is why disruption often begins at the bottom of the ladder, not the top.

Real-World Impact:

Domains hit:
Content writing, Call centers, Admin jobs, Backend ops, DevOps.

High-Risk Roles:
Content writing (short-form & templated), Call center agents & helpdesk operators, Routine admin & scheduling, Basic data entry & reporting, First-level IT monitoring

Job Perspective:
These tasks are expensive, repetitive, and fully digital. Easy to be replaced by AI.

Datapoints:
WEF's Future of Jobs Report 2023 states that roughly 44% of workers' core skills are expected to change within five years.

Future Perspective: A customer service rep in Manila watched the dashboard light up. By the time he moved his mouse, the AI had already resolved the ticket. He didn't know whether to feel amazed… or afraid.

* * *

Wave Two
Professions Under Reconstruction

Timeline: 1 Year –3 Years
(assumption based on how industries adapt and restructure around AI)

As the **second** wave builds, the disruption will move from tasks to roles. Entire functions will begin to reconfigure around AI capabilities - legal research, financial analysis, design, and even elements of teaching and healthcare.

Hybrid human–machine workflows will dominate, where the human role tilts toward oversight, judgment, and exception-handling rather than execution.

The next three years will be defined less by experimentation and more by restructuring, as industries adapt their operating models to integrate AI as a permanent layer in the value chain.

Real-World Impact:

Domain Hits:
Legal, education, finance, journalism, marketing, software development.

Likely to Shrink or Transform:
Paralegals & junior legal assistants, Financial analysts focused on routine modelling, Entry-level journalism & copy editing, Marketing campaign coordinators, Mid-level software developers.

Likely to Survive & Thrive:
Specialists in complex negotiations & courtroom litigation, Journalists in investigative or high-trust reporting, Creative directors & brand strategists, Senior engineers in systems architecture & integration

Job Perspective:
These roles have high ambiguity, judgment, or cultural context, in these areas AI still struggles with.

Datapoints:
McKinsey estimates up to 60–70% of tasks in data-heavy admin roles could be automated with existing technology.

Future Perspective: A 5th grader in Bengaluru asked his AI tutor to *"explain fractions with cricket."* The avatar smiled and said, *"Imagine a batsman scores ¼ of the total runs…"* He laughed. His teacher just watched, unsure whether to be proud or replaced.

* * *

Wave Three
The Deep Transformation

Timeline: 3 Years – 10 Years
(longer-term projection, dependent on policy, culture, and adoption speed)

The **third** wave will not simply touch tasks or roles but entire systems. Education, governance, and the labor market itself will confront structural changes. By this stage, AI will be embedded in decision-making processes, not just tools for productivity but engines of policy, strategy, and cultural influence.

The questions will no longer be about efficiency but about trust, authority, and accountability. This period, stretching from three to five years and beyond, will force society to reckon with the deeper consequences of AI's integration: not just how we work, but how we define human contribution and autonomy.

Real-World Impact:

Domain Hits:
Healthcare, architecture, R&D, engineering, leadership, arts.

Jobs Likely to Be Pressured:
Radiologists, pathologists (diagnostic heavy), Routine architectural drafting and structural design, Mid-tier R&D in

predictable domains, Middle management in process-driven organizations.

Jobs Likely to Endure:
Surgeons performing unpredictable, tactile procedures, Architects designing culturally rooted, context-specific spaces, Engineers solving novel, interdisciplinary problems, Leaders navigating complex human dynamics & ethics.

Job Perspective:
Physical unpredictability, cultural nuance, and high-stakes judgment are still human advantages, though the gap is narrowing. Require domain knowledge, but many routine parts can be automated.

Future Perspective: A surgeon reviews an AI-assisted scan and frowns. “I missed that… again.” He saves the patient.

* * *

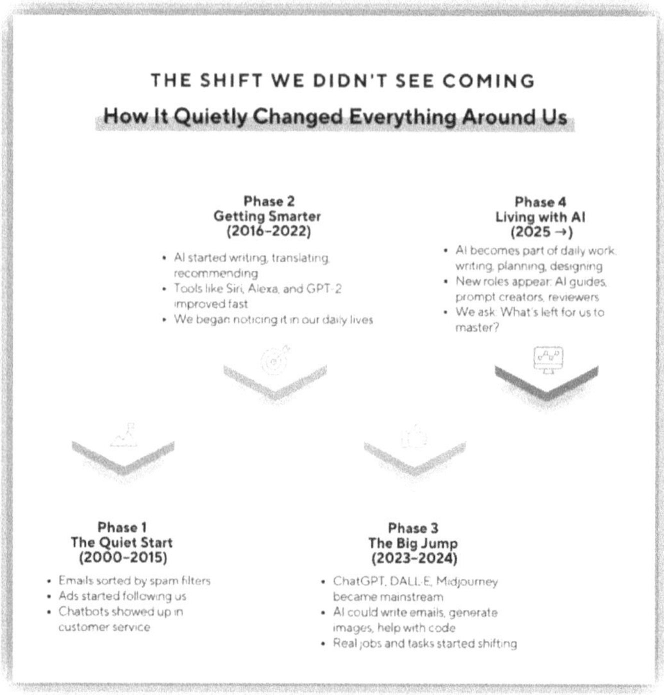

As AI moves up the ladder of cognition, humans must too. Not by resisting the climb, but by changing *how* and *why* we climb.

* * *

The Asymmetry of Disruption

But like every storm in history, this one didn't strike all lands equally.

In countries where labor is expensive, time is money, and digital infrastructure is mature, the wave of automation hits hard and fast.

In places like the United States, Western Europe, and Japan, AI doesn't just offer speed, it offers **economic relief**.

Why hire a team of content writers when one AI model drafts blog posts in minutes?
Why pay a legal assistant when AI reviews NDAs in seconds?
Why maintain an expensive support center when chatbots can handle 80% of queries?

Here, the pressure is not just about **innovation**. It's about **efficiency**.

But in other parts of the world like, India and Southeast Asia the wave is different.

Slower. Softer. More selective.

Because in economies where human labor remains affordable, replacing people isn't always the first or best option.

Here the value equation is different. People are not just workers; they are infrastructure. And AI, while powerful, still doesn't surpass the reliability of a human you can engage directly, face-to-face, at scale and with trust. So, in this world, the revolution waits at the gate… or walks in politely, step by step.

* * *

Part IV: Redefining the Human Edge

Realization

Seeing Through the Fog

Chapter 7

Fear Was Never the Ending

Fear begins the story, but adaptation writes the ending.

The world had been here before, shaken by something new, something vast, something it didn't yet understand.

When Gutenberg's printing press emerged in the 15th century, scribes cried foul. "*What will become of us?*" they asked, trembling at the idea that ink and gears could do in minutes what took them weeks.

But the **truth**? That invention sparked an era of mass literacy, democratized knowledge, and gave birth to revolutions in science, politics, and art.

Then came the Industrial Revolution. Machines took over manual labor. Hand-weavers lost their looms, and factories roared to life.

It was chaos, at first. But those who adapted found new trades, built new industries, and reshaped human civilization.

The **result**? Unprecedented growth, connected cities, and global trade.

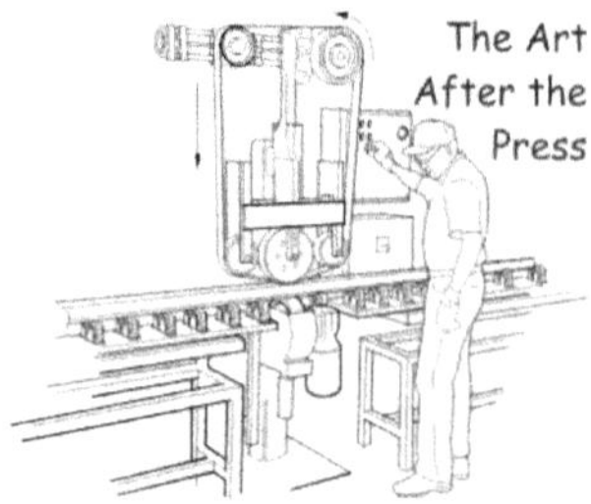

More recently, the digital age arrived. Computers replaced clerks. Emails threatened postal services. The Internet was once feared as a destroyer of bookstores, newspapers, and human attention.

Yet today, we marvel at how it connected the globe and empowered creators and businesses like never before.

And now… **AI**.

* * *

Not Replacement, but Redirection

AI is not the first disruptor, rather it may be the fastest. Its true impact lies not in erasing us, but in shifting where human effort creates value.

It absorbs what is procedural - translation, transcription, summarization - yet leaves untouched the realms of vision, invention, and meaning.

A teacher may lean on AI to generate lesson material but still stands irreplaceable in guiding curiosity.

A doctor may depend on AI to analyze scans but remains essential in judgment and empathy.

This is not a replacement. It is redirection - away from the mechanical, toward the distinctly human.

Yes, it is true, some work will be left behind. Just like the candle-maker's livelihood dimmed when electricity spread, but the world chose brightness over nostalgia.

If AI had a voice, it would be saying:
"*You don't need to do everything anymore.*
Let me carry the weight of the tasks. You carry the vision."

The fear of disappearance must give way to recognition of shift.

Yes, AI will unsettle professions, rewrite workflows, and demand new abilities. But it will not close the book on human worth.

Who's Really the Threat?

It's not the AI that takes your job. It's **you**, if you refuse to evolve.

Just like the ones who laughed at the internet, then begged for their job back. Just like the ones who dismissed digital banking, then waited in lines.

In every past disruption, those who adapted thrived. Those who resisted or dismissed the shift were overtaken.

The lesson is clear: it is not the presence of technology that displaces us, but our unwillingness to evolve alongside it.

This isn't an age of **extinction**. It's an age of **elevation** for those willing to step up.

* * *

Moving Forward

Fear is inevitable, but it is also temporary. Each revolution in work began with anxiety and ended with renewal. Printing spread ideas instead of silencing them. Industry expanded production instead of collapsing it. Computers birthed the digital age rather than ending the office.

History shows that humans do not vanish when tools advance. They change shape, redefine themselves, and find new forms of contribution. That truth holds now, though the disruption runs deeper.

Which brings us to the present. The question is no longer only whether fear will fade - it always has. The question is how it feels to live alongside this new mind, in the intimate reality of everyday life.

* * *

Chapter 8

Living with the Artificial Mind

Where machines assist, meaning remains ours.

There is a new rhythm now. Keystrokes click, alerts chime, and code runs silently in the background. Not the clang of hammers or the roar of engines, but the soft tap of keys echoing through digital spaces.

The day begins not with the sun alone, but with a familiar voice:
"Good morning. You have a 9 AM strategy sync, two emails flagged as urgent, and your heart rate is stable, perhaps a mindful walk before your next meeting?"

It's Alexa. Or Siri. Or Google. Or someone we never bothered to name yet trust more than our own memory.

Coffee machines talk. Fridges remind. Cars decide.
The human kingdom evolves not by hand, but by mind, sharpened with silicon.

Children no longer ask parents, *"What's the capital of Iceland?"*

Rather, they ask Alexa or ChatGPT or some other AI assistant.
Calendars are coordinated by algorithms.
Meals are planned by AI nutritionists.
Your car may soon sense your mood before your partner does.

But behind it all, still and always, there is choice. **Your choice.**

Because even in a world of infinite automation, it is, Humans who prompt, direct and care.

The machine may learn, but it does not dream.
It may respond, but it does not initiate meaning.

* * *

The Shared Mind

We live in a world where intelligence no longer belongs only to us. Every casual question - *"What's the weather?"* or *"Remind me to call Mom"* - is not just a command but an exchange.

Each prompt we give is a fragment of thought extended into a wider system, answered by a mind that is not our own yet feels seamlessly woven into our routines.

Once, tools were about strength. Later, they became about memory. Now, they are about thought itself.

A child asks an AI to explain fractions with football.

A teenager requests a playlist that mirrors a mood.
A family speaks to the fridge, and it answers with what is missing for dinner.
These are no longer tools waiting for instructions - they are companions anticipating the rhythm of life.

This is the quiet shift: intelligence has become shared. Some of it remains in us - curiosity, intent, meaning. Some of it rests in the system - pattern, scale, prediction. Neither side is complete on its own, but together they form a loop where human choice and machine suggestion constantly refine one another.

Even **today**, the act of thinking feels less solitary. We ask, it responds, and in its response, we discover new ways to phrase, to explore, to imagine. The line between where our thought ends and where the system begins is already blurred.

And **tomorrow**? That line will blur even further. Cars may adjust before we realize we are tired. Homes may dim the lights before we know we want to rest. Devices may sense frustration before we speak it aloud. Intelligence will not sit in a single place; it will surround us, ambient and anticipatory.

The question is no longer, *"Can machines think like us?"* but *"How do we think with them?"*

Because in this new age, intelligence is not a possession. It is a shared act, woven between human and system, intention and response.

Meaning still belongs to us. But intelligence, for the first time, is no longer ours alone.

The Dimensions of Existence

If intelligence can now be shared with machines, what about existence itself?

When we broadly visualize human existence, it is clear it cannot be reduced to the biological alone. We are not just bodies. We are also minds, moral agents, emotional beings, cultural creators, and seekers of meaning.

Existence unfolds in many dimensions. These are not universal categories, but a lens through which we might see ourselves. And on each of these planes, AI has begun to cast its reflection.

Biological existence has always been fragile: flesh, breath, and time. AI does not share this vulnerability, yet it increasingly shapes how we navigate it. From medical imaging that detects disease earlier than human eyes to genetic analysis that predicts risk, machines already influence our survival. In the future, they may even become partners in extending longevity, touching the boundaries of life once held only by biology.

Intellectual existence has long defined what it means to be human. We reason, imagine, and learn. AI now mirrors parts of that domain, predicting, calculating, and generating with fluency that challenges our role as the sole thinkers. Tomorrow, it may reshape not only what knowledge we value but also how we acquire it, raising the question: if machines can think with us, do we need to think differently?

Moral and ethical existence is more complex. Machines can simulate fairness, weigh outcomes, and suggest what seems "just." But they do not possess conscience. As AI systems guide decisions in courts, finance, and governance, the line between simulation and judgment may blur. The real concern is not whether AI will become moral, but whether our reliance on it will weaken our own vigilance.

Emotional and relational existence defines the bonds between us. AI companions can mimic empathy in words and gestures, offering comfort that feels convincing. In the future, they may play larger roles in caregiving, friendship, and even intimacy. Yet can relationships built with simulations ever carry the same weight as those forged through vulnerability and trust? The imitation may grow sharper, but the depth remains unreplicated.

Cultural and creative existence is where identity finds expression. Art, music, stories, and rituals form the pulse of humanity. AI already generates paintings, scripts, and songs with ease, and tomorrow it may weave entire cultural narratives. Yet creation without context lacks roots. Will future culture be co-authored with machines, or will it risk becoming a hall of mirrors, repeating patterns without history?

Existential and spiritual existence remains the furthest horizon. To ask *why we are here*, to search for meaning beyond function, has no counterpart in code. AI may process questions of purpose, even simulate wisdom, but it does not yearn. In the future, however, as people turn to machines for guidance, will spiritual authority itself be reshaped by artificial voices?

Across these dimensions, AI does not erase us. It reflects, extends, and unsettles what we call existence. The challenge is not only that machines touch these layers, but that we remember what cannot be replicated: the meaning of being.

* * *

Part V: The Age in Question

Exposure

The Truth We Stand On

Chapter 9

The Last Century Classroom

When the Syllabus Stays Still but the World Moves On.

The AI era is not waiting for permission. Workflows, industries, and even the definition of "skilled labor" are shifting in real time. Yet most classrooms remain anchored in an earlier age - designed for stability, not acceleration.

Graduates still step out of the ceremony with framed certificates and neatly packaged expertise, only to discover that the office they enter speaks a different language.

In the space between the classroom and the workplace, knowledge has aged. Not because it was wrong but because the world moved faster than the syllabus.

This isn't simply a **skills gap**. It's a **context gap**, a mismatch between how we prepare and how the game is now played.

An Education Built for Another Era

The architecture of formal education was forged in the industrial age.

Back then, a profession could rest on the same foundational tools for a decade without risk. Updating curricula every few years was enough.

In the AI economy, that cycle has collapsed. The functional shelf life of many technical skills is now **12–18 months**. By the time a committee approves a syllabus update, the tool it teaches may already be on version three or obsolete.

Policy cycles move slower than **product cycles**. Educators who have never used AI in their professional practice often teach it as an abstract concept, while industry treats it as baseline infrastructure.

And in many parts of the world, even where awareness exists, infrastructure lags too far behind to enable real adoption.

Yet many classrooms still prepare students for workflows that no longer exist, anchored to methods designed for a pre-AI economy.

Understanding about how AI systems function, where they fail, and how to work alongside them like prompt design, remains absent from much formal education.

The gap is no longer between theory and practice, but between relevance and obsolescence.

Thresholds of Tomorrow

Delay in adapting education and skills to the AI era is not neutral - it carries weighty consequences. The World Economic Forum projects that nearly **60% of the global workforce will need reskilling by 2030**, yet many may never receive it.

For individuals, the message is - "if your education did not prepare you for the AI age, waiting for the system to catch up could cost you years of relevance".

And yet, there are signals that transformation is possible. **Singapore** now treats AI literacy as foundational as mathematics, **Finland** frames it as a civic skill through its national course, and universities are embedding live AI projects into degree programs with partners like IBM, Microsoft, and Google. These are not widespread standards but important proofs of possibility.

The future of education, then, is poised between brink and bridge: delay widens the gap, but timely adoption offers a way forward. Whether societies fall behind or step ahead will depend on how quickly adaptation shifts from exception to norm - a tension that defines not only institutions but also the very roles we each hold in the age of intelligent machines.

***

Chapter 10

The Vulnerability Map

Mapping Job Exposure in the Age of Intelligent Machines.

The first time people hear that "*AI will change everything*" the instinctive question is personal: "*Will it change me?*". The honest answer is "*yes*". But not equally, not instantly, and not in the same way.

The future of your role depends on the type of work you do, the value it creates, and your willingness to evolve with the tools that are reshaping it.

From global research, *World Economic Forum (WEF)*, *McKinsey*, *OECD*, and *Microsoft's* AI Overlap Index (See Appendix, Ref-2) - job trajectories under AI pressure fall broadly into two categories – "High-Vulnerability Jobs" and "Resilience-with-Upskilling Jobs".

High-Vulnerability Jobs

These are roles where AI tools can already perform the bulk of the work faster, cheaper, and at acceptable quality for employers, like Customer service representatives, Financial analysts and so on. Mainly they share three traits:

— Digital (work is already on a computer).
— Repetitive (clear, rules-based processes).
— High-Volume (tasks that scale easily).

They're **at risk** because AI in these domains isn't experimental, it's proven, affordable, and increasingly integrated into standard software suites.

In high-cost economies, displacement pressure will be visible within **12–24 months**; in lower-cost regions, adoption will be slower but inevitable.

Resilience with Upskilling Jobs

These are roles that AI can ***assist*** but not ***replace***, provided the human evolve beyond baseline execution, like Senior legal professionals, Creative directors, Medical practitioners, Engineers and so on.

Without integrating AI literacy, these roles can slide toward vulnerability as AI tools grow more capable. The safe zone is not permanent. It's maintained through constant **renewal of skills**.

Vulnerability by Design, Resilience by Context

Exposure to AI is not uniform. Even within the same profession, the nature of tasks determines how quickly pressure arrives.

Roles rooted in **digital, repeatable, and rules-based processes** are the most fragile.

A **content writer** in New York, producing templated content, may find algorithms competing within months - tools that replicate tone, optimize for SEO, and deliver without fatigue.

By contrast, work grounded in **physical environments, cultural nuance, or unpredictable conditions** resists automation longer.

A truck **driver** navigating chaotic streets in Lagos, or a surgeon making tactile, high-stakes decisions, still operates in contexts machines cannot fully master.

That is why two people with the same job title may face radically different futures: one redefined by automation, the other safeguarded by context. Vulnerability is uneven, but it is also universal. The only variable is **when, not if**.

* * *

Put simply:

If work is expensive, repetitive, and digital, it's going first.
If work is local, physical, and nuanced, it's got some runway.

* * *

Relevance Starts with the Right Questions

To keep yourself relevant and future-ready, you need to do more than simply *know* about AI - you need to regularly audit your own position in the shifting landscape.

This starts with asking the right type of questions and evaluating the answers honestly. The goal is not to judge yourself, but to uncover where action is needed.

Ask yourself:

"Can AI tools already do 50% or more of my routine tasks?"

"If AI took over the repetitive parts of my job tomorrow, would I still add unique value?"

"Do I regularly experiment with AI tools relevant to my field?"

"Have I learned skills that AI can't yet master like negotiation, cultural nuance, systems thinking?"

Your **answers** will reveal whether you are positioned for growth, at risk of stagnation, or in danger of replacement.

Before you assume the worst or the best about your role, it's worth seeing how AI has performed so far when put to the test.

* * *

Part VI: Beyond the Illusion

Clarity

Where Hype Ends and Clarity Begins

Chapter 11

Between Hype and Reality

Where AI's Promise Meets the Limits of the Real World.

When AI first hit the mainstream, the predictions came fast and loud. Developers would vanish. Drivers would disappear. Writers, lawyers, teachers, all replaced by a tide of silicon intelligence.

The narrative was simple: "*machines can now do what we do, so what's left for us?*"

But reality has been more measured. The question now is how much of the AI storm is mere wind, and how much is the wave.

AI has changed work, sometimes dramatically but it has not erased the human hand. Not yet, and not entirely.

* * *

Software Development

One of the earliest claims was that generative AI could write entire software applications without a human developer. **Reality?** AI-powered coding assistant tools like GitHub Copilot have indeed transformed the developer's workflow but not by replacing them.

Most studies put productivity gains at **10–30%**, not 100%. AI can draft code, but it still stumbles without human guidance on many things like Context, Architecture, Trade-offs.

In the Software Development Life Cycle (SDLC), AI shines at repetitive, well-defined tasks, but cannot replace the nuanced decision-making and domain understanding that humans bring.

***

Self-Driving Cars

The promise of fully autonomous vehicles was supposed to be "just a few years away" - for the last decade. Reality has been stubborn.

While Level 2 and Level 3 autonomy (adaptive cruise control, lane keeping, traffic jam assist) are widely available, Level 5 - true, driverless freedom, remains elusive.

Why? Because roads are unpredictable. AI can handle 99% of scenarios flawlessly but the last **1%** contains everything from a child chasing a ball into traffic to a temporary road closure with no clear signage. That 1% is where human adaptability still wins.

***

Content Generation

Yes, AI can produce blog posts, ad copy, and even scripts in seconds. But "fluent" does not equal "compelling." Left unguided, AI-generated content can be bland, repetitive, or subtly off in tone.

It lacks true originality, merely rearranging patterns it has already seen, often struggles with emotional nuance unless carefully guided, and frequently misses the context-specific hooks that make a message resonate with its intended audience. In marketing, publishing, and journalism, AI is best seen as a **first draft machine**, freeing humans to focus on refinement, storytelling, and strategic messaging.

***

Customer Service

Chatbots have become capable of handling high volumes of customer queries, often faster and more consistently than human agents.

But their competence has clear limits; when a question falls outside their training data, they cannot improvise. They struggle to sense unstated needs or emotional cues as a skilled human agent would. They can deliver correct answers to the wrong problem because they miss the deeper "why" behind a customer's request.

For complex, customized, or high-stakes interactions, humans remain indispensable.

* * *

Why Reality Lags the Hype

The gap between AI's promise and AI's impact isn't because the technology is weak, it's because the world it operates in is messy.

Contexts shift. Data is incomplete. Human behavior refuses to fit neat patterns.

AI thrives where the environment is structured, rules are clear, and outcomes are measurable. Everywhere else, human adaptability, empathy, and judgment are still the edge.

The truth is that AI is neither the unstoppable conqueror some feared, nor the harmless gadget others hoped for.

* * *

Chapter 12

Steering Through Uncertainty

The path ahead is unclear. But with the right questions, we can find our way.

In every period of transformation, humanity has sought a way to navigate, not to predict outcomes, but to act with intent when the familiar gives way to the unknown. What distinguishes this moment is the speed and reach of the change.

Artificial Intelligence is not a single invention, but an expanding system altering the mechanics of work, the nature of decision-making, and the frameworks through which societies define value. The question is no longer whether it will affect us, but how do we choose to respond while the ground is still moving.

From Reaction to Adaptation

Traditional patterns of adoption, where innovation is followed by gradual integration and eventual standardization, no longer apply.

AI evolves in weeks, not years, with each update altering the skills, systems, and policies required to manage it.

Reskilling cycles that once matched the pace of change now lag dangerously behind, and regulations often arrive after the technology has already reshaped the terrain.

The only viable posture is one of continuous adaptation, where learning, unlearning, and recalibration are part of the daily rhythm rather than exceptional events.

* * *

Reorienting Education for the AI Era

This shift demands more than operational skills. Closing the gap between syllabus and real world will require more than adding an "AI Basics" course to existing programs. AI literacy should be woven into every discipline, from engineering and law to art and sociology.

There could be two possible futures - **one path** leads to graduates stepping into the workforce with credentials but without relevance, spending their first years catching up instead of contributing.

The **other** produces professionals who can adapt to any AI model or tool not because they have memorized its functions, but because they understand its purpose, its limits, and its place in the wider system.

The choice is not only for policymakers or educators to make. It is a societal choice, one that determines whether education prepares for the world as it is or clings to the world as it was.

***

The Geopolitics of Intelligence

AI is not only a technical force; it is geopolitical. Nations investing early in infrastructure, education, and regulation are likely to gain lasting economic and strategic advantage, while those that lag risk dependence on systems they did not design.

Yet the same capabilities that drive innovation can also enable surveillance, concentrated control, and the manipulation of information. The trajectory is neither predetermined nor neutral, and governance will be as decisive as invention.

***

Redefining Progress and Purpose

The arrival of systems that can match or exceed human performance in certain domains forces a reconsideration of what it means to contribute.

AI can take the repeatable and the scalable; humans must retain the contextual, the ethical, and the creative under ambiguity.

Progress will be measured less by speed or efficiency, and more by the ability to direct these capacities toward the right ends.

Purpose will no longer rest in static roles, but in the capacity to create value in shifting conditions while holding to principles that endure.

In this changing world, we each need to find and regularly recalibrate our own compass. Not to resist change, but to meet it with clarity. Because the future will not just happen to us. It will be shaped by the questions we ask, the decisions we make, and the values we choose to carry forward.

***

Epilogue

The Unfinished Story

The next chapter waits for the choices we make.

So here we are. Not at an end. But at a crossing. A time where the *old world*, forged in flesh, fire, and friction meets a *new world* shaped by invisible codes and unblinking minds.

We've walked through the arc of wonder, conflict, disruption, fear, and displacement. We have lived with uncertainty, sought clarity, and now, we stand at the doorway of **possibility**.

But not everything is answered. Nor should it be.
The questions we leave behind:
As AI writes for us, plans for us, drives for us, thinks with us:
"Will our own skills sharpen or soften?".
"Will we rise higher, freed to create, dream, and solve more?

Or will we drift into comfortable dependency, losing the very edge that once defined us?”.

If we no longer calculate, recall, or organize on our own, do we lose our grip on those muscles?

History reminds us, every tool that replaced muscle gave us more time to think.
Now, tools that replace thinking might give us more time to feel, connect, and imagine - if we choose to use them that way.

The human mind is not gone but it no longer stands alone.
If AI can do the work, we must do the wondering.
If it can solve the problem, we must decide which problems matter.

The next chapter of this story is unwritten.
It will not be authored by algorithms alone, nor by humans alone, but by both together. The pen is still in our hands. The question is: **What will we choose to write?**

***

Postscript

If this book has challenged your thinking or given you more clarity on the role of AI in our future, I invite you to share your thoughts in the form of an Amazon review.

Your perspective matters - not only to me as the author but to readers who are deciding whether this journey is worth taking.

A few sentences are enough. Maybe you can share with others what you discovered, questioned, or saw differently.

Your words will help shape the broader conversation about AI's place in our world.

Thank you for reading and for contributing to the dialogue this book was written to begin.

— **Bhaskar Deb**

Appendix

Ref-1: Your Compass for the AI Era

This book ends, but your journey with AI does not. The following is not a checklist or a strategy playbook. Think of it as a compass, something you can return to whenever the landscape feels uncertain, and you need direction.

1. Perspectives to Hold

How you see the world will shape how you act in it. These perspectives aren't optional; they are survival mindsets for the age of intelligent machines.

- **Co-Creation, Not Competition**
  Don't ask, *"Will AI replace me?"* Ask instead, *"How can I lead with it?"*
- **Adaptability Over Expertise**
  What you know matters less than how quickly you can learn.
- **Purpose Over Productivity**
  AI can do the tasks. You must define why the tasks matter.

2. Practices to Keep

Daily habits that will keep you relevant, resilient, and aware.

- **Work With AI, Not for It**
  Treat AI as a collaborator you're still learning to trust. Use it, question it, and teach it how you think.

- **Interrogate the Output**
  Don't just consume what AI produces. Ask why, refine, and make the final call your own.

- **Pause Before Decisions**
  AI is fast, but your clarity is the differentiator. Reflection, not speed, defines wisdom.

3. Edges to Sharpen

These are not just "skills" but enduring human strengths that will keep you distinct.

- **The Art of Asking Better Questions**
  In an AI world, fluency belongs to those who know how to prompt, probe, and challenge.

- **Human-First Communication**
  Empathy, storytelling, and nuance are your signature. Algorithms can mimic tone but not intent.

- **Systems Thinking**
  See beyond the task. Understand connections, consequences, and the bigger design.

4. Guardians of Human Value

Every profession carries a human responsibility - something no algorithm can fully inherit. Here's what different roles must guard in the years ahead:

- **Leaders** → Direction and governance.
- **Educators** → Curiosity and critical thinking.
- **Creatives** → Originality and voice.
- **Healthcare professionals** → Empathy and trust.
- **Managers** → Judgment and ethics.
- **Students** → Adaptability and imagination.

These are not just skills - they are responsibilities. If humans let go of them, machines will not pick them up. They will simply disappear.

Ref-2: Understanding AI Core Concepts

A quick reference guide to ideas explored in this book

Concept	What It Means
Neural Networks	Digital structures inspired by the brain, processing patterns through layered "neurons."
Machine Learning (ML)	Algorithms that learn from data and improve without explicit reprogramming.
Deep Learning	Multi-layered ML, excels at recognizing images, speech, and patterns in massive data.
Generative AI	Models that create text, images, code, and music based on learned patterns.
Foundation Models	Large-scale models (e.g., GPT) trained broadly, adaptable to many domains.
Natural Language Processing (NLP)	AI's ability to understand and generate human language.
Reinforcement Learning (RL)	Trial-and-error learning with feedback "rewards."
AI Overlap Index	Microsoft's 'AI applicability score,' or what we call the 'AI Overlap Index,' measures how much of a role AI can take on.

About the Author

Bhaskar Deb is a Solution Architect and Technology Leader with two decades of experience guiding Fortune 100 companies through digital transformation and AI adoption. His work bridges technical expertise with human-centered insight, guiding leaders through both the promise and the peril of technology.

In *AI The Uninvited Mind*, he extends this perspective, tracing the rise of artificial intelligence as more than a story of progress. It is a force colliding with human meaning, cultural identity, and the fragile balance between work, life, and what it means to remain human.

www.ingramcontent.com/pod-product-compliance
Lightning Source LLC
LaVergne TN
LVHW052115210926
848482LV00025B/656